# HUGGING DEATH

*Essays on Motherhood and Saying Goodbye*

## JEAN KNIGHT PACE

Copyright © 2018 by Jean Knight Pace

All rights reserved.

No part of this book may be reproduced in any form or by any electronic or mechanical means, including information storage and retrieval systems, without written permission from the author, except for the use of brief quotations in a book review.

*To my mother. Here's hoping for an eternity of laughter.*

I'd like to thank the publications in which several of these essays originally appeared:

*A Cup of Comfort for Mothers*

*We Will Survive*

*Legends and Legacies*

## CONTENTS

| | |
|---|---|
| Author's Note | ix |
| Rings | 1 |
| Likenesses | 12 |
| Wayward Cells | 15 |
| Undressing the Dead | 21 |
| Hugging Death | 26 |
| About the Author | 31 |

## Author's Note

These essays, as you'll see, are quite personal. And my mom didn't get to have any say in them. I'm not entirely sure my mother would approve of every detail in every essay.

When you are dying, there are many pieces of indignity. Yet it is within some of that indignity that we often find grace. It is in some of that indignity that children sometimes finally have the chance to serve their parents in ways parents spent years serving their children. That's what dying parents hate so much about it—becoming the child. And yet, for me, that is where so much of the intimacy, the beauty, comes in.

I hope that if my mother is reading this over my

shoulder, she will forgive me for some of the sentences in some of the essays, and that she will see the small snatches of grace and beauty that she showed me.

# Rings

WE CALL MY MOTHER WHEN I AM IN LABOR. "TELL her she has to come this weekend," I instruct Kip from the hospital bed.

"Jean wants to know if you can come this weekend."

"No," I correct him. "Tell her she must take Friday off and come this weekend."

In the end she can only get half a day off so she won't get from Utah to Colorado until Friday night. I'm irritated that a stupid long-term sub job gets priority over the birth of her first grandchild. And me.

---

WHEN I WAS TWENTY-TWO WE BOUGHT HER A

mother's ring. Five stones: emerald, ruby, garnet, rose zircon, green tourmaline. Jean, Rebecca, Katie, Jake, Barry. She wore it on her hand in place of the half-carat diamond she'd put back in its box a year earlier—unsure of what to do with it now that my father was part of a different state, religion, lifestyle. What do you do with a large diamond, with a twenty-three year history, with five children and two dogs?

---

When she arrives she's brought my memory box—my old teddy bear, the Cabbage Patch doll she made me, yellow and green afghans, the clothes I wore when I was small.

Mark sits at my breast, detached, blowing milky breath onto the wet nipple. I watch his face. I tell her it amazes me how much it can change—the lips pulling down into a frown, then circling around into a tiny *O*; the folds of skin creasing inward like his face wants to crack; the way his eyebrows shoot up as if he is a very old man; how the corner of his mouth reaches into a toothless half smile against my chest.

She tells me how she used to watch my expression for hours. She tells me people used to come up to her in stores and ask if they could pet my dandelion hair.

She pulls a red jumper out of the memory box and tells me that this is the outfit I'm wearing in the picture where I stand in the sink with a bottle of cleanser. Mark sleeps and she empties the memory box onto the floor of his room.

---

DAD PROPOSED BY BAKING A CHECK INTO A CAKE. For months, he'd been telling her he was going to the library to study, and working a third job on the sly to make enough money for a ring—digging feces out of clogged pipes so she could have a diamond bigger than he could afford. Mom bought herself a round, deep stone looped with gold and attached to a thin band.

---

"I'M OUT OF PRACTICE," MOM SAYS, WRAPPING THE diaper deftly and firmly around Mark's waist. Kip and I inspect the diaper like she has just performed a bit of magic. We have not yet been able to produce more than a sad, sagging thing, crooked, loose at his hips and tight around the legs. Hers is a masterpiece—a well-crafted piece of remembered experience.

I think about the summer Barry was born and then two days later Bec, Jake, and I got the chicken pox and then two weeks later we moved from Pennsylvania to Ohio. I think of my mother packing our house into neat boxes and making us chocolate chip milkshakes because the chicken pox lined our lips and mouths and throats.

When school started I wrote about it in my "What I Did for Summer Vacation" paper. To my eleven-year-old mind, it was funny.

I hadn't realized then what it meant for a body to have a baby—the first few days of heavy blood, the vulva that swells so that sitting, standing, and walking are painful, the hemorrhoids, the hormonal shifts, the sore breasts, the sleeplessness. I hadn't realized what it meant to pack a household into neat brown boxes while the body feels all that, or how it would be to do it without the help of an ultra-busy husband and with children underfoot. I didn't think one single time when I asked for another milkshake with extra chocolate chips or complained about taking a baking soda bath that she might have been tired or sad or in pain.

I think about it now, and that June grows incomprehensible to me.

---

IN THE MORNING, I DRAG TO THE ROOM WHERE Mom is staying. "Take him. Kip and I have to get some sleep." She lies on her back on the air mattress. He curls up on her chest, his legs and arms tucked under him—like he hasn't yet realized he's left the warmth of a mother.

---

THE NIGHT BEFORE MY WEDDING I SLEPT WITH Mom in her bed. I don't remember why. I suppose there were too many siblings in other beds. Or perhaps it was just comfortable and warm and safe—her patting my arm and back as I shifted sleeplessly through the night. Mom—able to let me go, give me to a man—three daughters in three years. Mom—strong enough to push me out of herself, to give me over to someone else to be weighed, measured, swaddled, and taken away.

I kept my ring on that night—something small but dense that I could close my hand on and feel—something to remind me that negligence and betrayal would not creep into our lives like they had with her and Dad—something compact and heavy, like a solid foreign coin.

---

WE USED TO PLAY WITH DAD'S WEDDING BAND. I remember sitting in church and embossing rings onto my palm. Mom says that's how it got lost—he let us play with it in the car once and then it was gone, out the window she supposed.

She kept hers on always—when she washed the dishes, slept, showered. She kept it on through Dad's medical school, through all of our births, through Dad's lost business dream, through all the things that would have made other women take it off. She kept it on so long that when the divorce proceedings began, she was worried it wouldn't slide over the widened knuckle and she'd have to have it cut off.

---

MY MOTHER IS BRAVE AND CERTAINLY STRONG. IT'S something I do not envy. Because only experience can grant it. I want the right to be just a little fragile, a little weak, a little less than the superwoman Mom was expected, and later—through divorce—forced to become.

---

THE YEAR BARRY TURNED TEN WAS THE YEAR DAD became obsessed with the Internet, the year he started seeing other people.

Mom told me that until that year, the worst year of her life had been a long time ago—when she'd had the first of a series of miscarriages, gotten pregnant again, and then miscarried the second child on the day the first was supposed to be born.

---

THREE YEARS AFTER MY FATHER'S FIRST LEAVING, Kip proposed to me by slipping a ring onto my finger while I lay with my eyes closed next to him on a picnic blanket. That night we went to Mom's house with the announcement. She said something like, "Oh, that's nice."

After Kip was gone, I accused her of not being happy for me. She told me she had expected the proposal—that's why she wasn't more excited—because it wasn't a surprise. I hoped I believed her.

She cuddles Mark upstairs while Kip and I stay down in the kitchen and pay bills. By the fridge, Kip puts his arms all the way around my middle and laughs, saying, "Hey, they fit."

It feels divine.

---

Before I was engaged, before I was even quite sure that I wanted to be, I used to go into Mom's room and try on her boxed wedding ring—admire the shape of my hands and nails and how well it all looked with that ring. I used to imagine how, if things had gone differently, she might have given the ring to me—passed it down to her eldest daughter.

As it is, I don't want her ring. Don't want the reminders of their broken union. I'm already reminded enough—when Mom can't find a job she wants because of her age and inexperience; when she tells me about this dance she went to and how a weird guy named Floyd kept asking her to dance and it's like she's fourteen again; when there are nights that I can feel the heat from Kip's body beside me, but can't fill the space between us because we've disagreed about something and it seems that if I press too close, he will leave me.

---

Religiously, I believe in love and marriage through eternity. There is no "till death do us part" in our wedding ceremonies. We believe in a ring of husbands and wives, brothers and sisters, sealed forever. But we also do not believe in forcing people to stay in the circle, so sometimes people choose to step out, break the band, which is what happens with a divorce.

I've always hated those wedding rings that sometimes come as part of a set—the ones that don't make a full circle, that leave a little gap where the two tips of metal don't quite meet. They make them that way so a diamond engagement ring can be fitted in. Practical and stylish and void of the symbol that's so important to me.

---

Sunday morning Mom sits on the bed. I sit across from her in the rocking chair with Mark on my lap. She's got to leave after lunch to make the drive back to Utah before she gets too tired. My first child and I've had her for only forty-one hours.

It cuts a sadness into me, an envy for friends whose mothers come for weeks and sometimes longer, friends with unbroken families, with non-working mothers.

---

She calls me that night when she gets home and tells me she's tired, but well. She also tells me my brother's car is on the fritz so she'll have to share her car with Jake so he can get to work. Which means she won't be able to come again in a couple of weekends like I'd hoped she would. She's sorry. I tell her it's fine, that I understand. And I do, except when I don't.

---

I told my mother a few months before Mark was born that I was still afraid of the dark—that when Kip has to work all night I leave about four lights on and sometimes listen to children's Sunday school songs for comfort before I go to bed.

Mom told me that was normal, that lots of women

are like this, that the other doctors' wives she knew used to get freaked out when their husbands had to be on call overnight.

But Mom didn't. She had five kids and was never afraid.

When I was ten, we all came home one night to find a bat flying loops through the living room. Dad ordered us kids to wait outside in the dark. We stood in a line on the sidewalk and watched the square of light that came through the pale curtains of the living room. We heard Dad screech—high and shrill.

Mom killed the bat with a broom.

---

Two days after my mother leaves, Kip goes back to work. I still leave a light on, but not exactly because I am afraid. I leave it on so that I can find my way to Mark's bassinet, so that I can watch his tiny face with the fists balled up by his head. So that I can see my son, and be a little bit of the brave my mother was.

# Likenesses

Whether you try to or not, there are pieces of your mother you can't avoid: moments when you walk past a mirror and see a bit of her looking back at you; when you hear in your laugh a tone that is not wholly your own; when you walk into your house to see a corner of it looking like a corner of hers.

I have my hands—holding a book, a brush, a spoon. When I look down it's like seeing her: same big veins, same knobby knuckles, petite fingers, strong lines, fingernails that curve in ways that would make a manicurist cringe.

And I have an unruly pile of books stacked on the dresser by my bed. I clean it occasionally. For a day or two my dresser is neatly sparse. And then an article catches my attention. It reminds me of an essay. And before long I've added that book I haven't finished, the parent reference I wanted to read again, *10,001 Best Baby Names*, my notebook, my journal, scraps of paper, a seashell from my daughter. Pieces of me like reflections of her.

And I treasure them—these likenesses, messy and imperfect, like living memories.

---

SHE IS DYING OF CANCER. I AM LIVING WITH FOUR small bundles of life called children. She is winding down, getting her affairs in order. I am winding up—preparing for elementary school, teenagers, college, marriages, and trying to figure out what exactly my affairs are. Sometimes she visits—bald and stumbling, with only one small suitcase and a best-seller from the airport in tow. And I wonder—with my house full to bursting with children's clothes, toys, sleeping bags, art work; and my hands full to bursting with cooking, gardening, teaching, and accounting—how will we know each other, how will we remember each other, when she is gone?

Then I lift a pen to write a check and I see her there in the lines on my thumb and in the veins that pull down to my wrist. I see in me the age coming on, and know how that hand will look in ten, twenty, thirty years. I hear her too—every morning when I reach for the alarm and a fumble of books shifts and slides, the top magazine slipping to the floor, the tower clanking down next to my jewelry box.

It is then that I remember how she was when young—her own brood of children even bigger than mine—the messy, cold kitchen, our from-scratch birthday cakes, the homemade cabbage patch doll, piano lessons, pre-dawn Christmas mornings. I remember climbing into bed with her after I got home from a date, her early morning smell, the look of her in a nightgown.

And I hope that in the months to come, when I fold my hands or re-stack my books and my mother jumps out at me from myself, I'll be able to forget her body betraying itself, the home health nurses, the stream of bad news, the passing. I hope that I'll think simply of her and know that her soul will smile to see my hands as hers, and the same mound of books at my bedside.

Wayward Cells

Everyone's mother is dead or dying. It is nothing new, nothing ceasing, nothing fresh or interesting. But when *your* mother is dying and when this dying insists at once that you take notice of it, you feel her bones in your own and that insistence stretches into the vision you have of your own life.

---

My mother hobbles from her condo to the pool. Her key is attached to a bracelet on her wrist. Her hair is mostly gone on one side of her head. Her skin is warm but loose. She insists on speech, but none of it comes out in the way she intends. To compensate, I ramble on about the things in our life: the kids, the ducks, the house. And my children swirl like bees, eager to swim, to vacation with Grandma, to run up the stairs of the condo. They love the wigs she rarely bothers to wear anymore, the cane that rests by her door. They love sick Grandma as much as whole Grandma. In fact, I'm not really sure they're aware of the difference.

Sometimes I envy them because I feel the difference acutely. On this trip I feel it more than usual, and realize that through our weekly phone calls Mom has concealed much of her decline from me. Or perhaps it has just come up on her in a rush as the tumor in the side of her brain crowds out the woman who is my mother.

My mother and I have always been close. Not in the girly ways some women connect. We have never once done each others' nails, or even considered it. We have shopped together only out of necessity and with the pragmatic efficiency of small town women for whom the mall is an hour away.

But I have always been a good talker and she has always held an open ear. It made for a good match. In my almost completely innocent days of high school and college, I told her nearly everything. Back then, in her faithful looking to bright future days, she listened and even told me some of her own life.

Which, for my mother, was not the type of thing that poured out with ease.

Now I talk of weather, of treatments, of complicated drug names. Now my mother sits by the pool—a stone wall bleached white by the sun.

Her future is to be cut short, her present a confusing and uncomfortable place in which to stand, and her past shadowed a bit too darkly by cloudy days for her to well remember the achingly sunny ones.

As if in cruel punishment for her complaints, the tumor in her brain winds into her speech—verbs, tenses, and rules of grammar once so carefully observed are cast aside by the tentacles of wayward cells. Her word order changes as though translated by a computer from a foreign tongue. And thoughts my mother is quite lucid enough to think refuse to take shape into clauses and participles, vowels and consonants lined up properly in the words she does utter.

In the weeks just before my arrival in Utah, phone conversation had become difficult, almost impossible. We'd continued on as gracefully as we could, even as Mom's words crumbled into heaps I could not properly assemble.

Now, here with her—sitting together on her porch on

an overcast evening, my husband and children engaged in a game of hide and seek—here the silences and disconnects do not weigh so much and we can enjoy each other a bit more as mother and daughter should. But we will have this face-to-face camaraderie for only a few worrisome days before I fly back over state after state, and the phone—while she can still operate it—becomes our only recourse.

---

AND ALL THE WHILE, I CONTINUE TO DIE TOO—not in the solid way of a woman harboring a brain tumor, but in the way that we are all dying—slowly, surely, and mostly imperceptibly. Here in my mid-thirties, watching my mother decline, it seems much more palpable than it did fifteen years ago. Now it's easier to see the way my brain refuses to find a word it knows, or to put that word in the right place when I'm tired, easier to see the forced quiet that this could eventually become.

To watch thirty-, forty-, fifty-something actresses with their clever television quips, their careers laid out in the steely feminism that promises protection from dependence and decline, their breasts and faces propped up with plastic and creams and lasered invasions—to see these women is not to think of dying.

To see these women is to see a careful scaffold built against age itself.

But to hold my mother's hand—a hand that used to be as solid and strong as eternity, and to feel the skin soft and thin, to feel the lack of muscle one does not realize a hand possesses until it is gone, to know that the control and use of that hand is now limited by the erratic waves neurally transmitted to it—to see this is to see the ashes I will become.

And while I, of a religious nature, do not inherently fear ash or dust, it's easier to accept with calmness and patience when it belongs to an unrelated someone's life cycle.

---

I cannot do the "warm up" Sudoku puzzle I hold in my lap. I feel I must master it before the plane ride home ends—must reassure myself that the synapses are still firing and connecting. But when, near the end, two sevens blink at me from the same row, I scratch a heavy line through it and we land.

My mother calls to see if we returned safely. Her words line up correctly and I tell her that we have. I might as well stand up and sing because knowing she can still call me on the phone does something for me.

The next day I steal my nine-year-old's Sudoku book and work for forty-five minutes on the one titled "Very Easy." It's well past my bedtime when I conquer it, but I feel a small tinge of relief. There is still life left to grab. For me. And, in these last precious months, for her.

## Undressing the Dead

❦

WOMEN HAVE ALWAYS BEEN THE KEEPERS OF THE dead. We have washed the bodies, anointed with oils and herbs, clothed for burial, paid our last respects in that final rite that has ever been our own.

I wanted to make the special request to be allowed to dress my mother. Ever since it had become clear that she would not miraculously recover from her brain tumor, I had wanted to do this. I had dreaded it too, but not as much as I had wanted to be with my mother in what I considered her final hour. I had wanted to give her a gift daughters have given their mothers for more generations than I can fathom. I braced for the scene—the clothes draped carefully around her body, the delicate and careful way my sisters and I would handle this precious woman, the memories we would speak of, the gentle tears we would shed. I could practically touch this memory I hadn't yet made.

But Utah state law couldn't. My mother would be dressed by a licensed mortician. I could add a few final touches at the end.

My mother's mortician was a bubbly gray-haired man named Joe who couldn't stop admiring the make-up job he'd given my mother. He made small talk like a pro, even when handling a body that had taken its last breath several days before. A unique skill set and one that I did not possess.

My job was to add a sash and a veil to her outfit. I had never in my life touched a dead person, much less moved one around. The closest I'd actually come to a bona fide corpse was the elderly neighbor I'd once found lying next to his house—a leaf blower on the ground next to him. I'd driven past him at first and then I'd stopped and backed up. It seemed odd that someone would take a nap right by their house with a discarded leaf blower. Very odd. I got out of my car. His chest didn't rise or fall. His skin was very pale. His mouth open. I called my husband—a paramedic—who hurried over and went right to the body. Touched wrist and neck, shone the light from his keychain flashlight into the eyes. Quite dead, he'd pronounced. I was still twenty feet from the body, standing on the edge of the lawn like a skulking dog.

My mother's body lay in front of me—much less foreign than the neighbor I didn't know, but just as dead. Her hand was cold. I had expected cool. Cool I could imagine. Cool was my hands and feet every night when I burrowed them into my husband's warm skin. Cool was the icy way they felt when we got home after a morning of sledding. Cool was something that could get so bad that sometimes it hurt. Mom's hand didn't hurt. Because cool was not cold. Cold was something I hadn't felt before in human flesh. Cold was my mother.

That same hand had been immobile for months. Immobile, but alive. Just two weeks earlier my sister-in-law and I had gone to her house and her hand had been hanging over her bed. It had swelled so big that the ring on that finger seemed it would soon cut into the skin. Mom couldn't feel it. But when I held the hand—massaging the blood and fluids away from her finger and then lotioning her hand for several minutes until, finally, I could maneuver the ring off—it had been warm. It had been my mother.

The woman who was now laid out in front of me was not. The carefully dressed and arranged body was the shell of my mother, the case—something to say goodbye to after the spirit had fled—a vestige almost, a memento of the woman who once was. I was not afraid to touch her, exactly, but touching her reminded me of what this body wasn't.

Joe-the-chatty-mortician had no such qualms about my mother. He talked with me about burial clothes and showed me how to slide the sash underneath my mother, shift the body so I didn't have to bear its full weight. He did most of it. I shivered and sniffled. My sister reached out and touched Mom's hand for just an instant—like a child might have—then pulled back and cried on my brother's shoulder, the kid parts and grown up parts of us all mixed up.

My mother's body was dressed and nearly ready. She would need a wig still. The chemo had worn away her once-beautiful hair. And then the veil. Her husband put her wedding ring onto her finger. He planned to have her buried with it. On her other hand—the hand I had massaged—was her mother's ring.

My siblings and I had decided we would keep it. It was silly, my brother said, to bury something valuable—a point on which all the siblings could agree, and a fact it seemed our mother would have whole-heartedly supported. But in our discussion of the ring, none of us had determined who exactly the *we* was that would keep it.

Just before they closed the coffin, the mortician handed me the ring. I had no purse or pockets, and so I slipped it onto my right finger. Where it fit perfectly. I hadn't expected in that small artifact, undressed from my mother's cold hand, to find a piece of her, to get a touch of her back.

And yet, there it was. The ring that was perfectly my size on the fingers that were just like my mother's had been twenty-five years ago when we had given it to her.

My mother wasn't there, in her perfectly dressed body wearing more make-up than she had probably ever owned in the entirety of her life. But my mother was there in me—in my hands and body, in my habits and laugh. She was there in my siblings, in our children, in all the memories we held of her. Seeing her hands through my hands was haunting, and yet weirdly comforting. My hand was alive. My hand was her hand given to me. My hand was a reminder of all the things she'd done with her hands over the years—of warmth and cool.

Of life.

## Hugging Death

My stepfather, Jay, went to get groceries. Almost as soon as he was gone, my mother motioned to me that she had to go to the bathroom, an insistent point at the plastic toilet, a frustrated grunt—like a two-year-old in the urgency and inconvenience of her timing.

I had never helped an adult go to the bathroom. The night before, I'd seen just a snatch of Jay helping her get back into bed after using the portable adult-sized toilet that sat beside the bed. So little dignity in that big potty, but more than she had in diapers, and she insisted on using it.

I helped her sit up, swung her legs over the side of the bed, and positioned her feet squarely on the floor. She had only panties on her bottom half—the same kind the hospital gives you just after you have a baby —and I wasn't quite sure how I would get them off when the time came. She wrapped her one good arm around my shoulder while her other hung limp. Bending at my knees, I pulled her up off the bed. I consider myself strong for a woman, but my mother —completely unable to use one of her legs and extremely limited in her use of the other—was a hundred and fifty pounds of dead weight.

I took a step nearer to the toilet, and then my balance wavered. Standing together, our arms wrapped around each other, the two of us swayed like a tall building blown in the wind. I pictured myself dropping my mother—her head knocking on the floor or the end table before her husband returned, before any of my siblings arrived to say their goodbyes. Maybe she was picturing that too, because she held on tight with that one good arm. I held on tight with both of mine—a big, involuntary bear hug as we wobbled between adult-sized potty and bed. And then, with her bottom half mostly exposed, swaying with me in that sad little slow dance, my mother started to laugh.

I laughed too, because it was better than crying, and once the laughter started we grabbed onto it like we held onto each other.

Her laugh—it was the same one she'd always had, the very same laugh. Maybe she couldn't talk well; maybe her words came out in hackneyed phrases that I couldn't always piece together; maybe her handwriting and spelling were long gone. But her laugh was just like it had been all those years of my life. The brain cancer couldn't steal it.

Somehow, I inched over to the potty and, with more of a plunk than I would have liked, I set her on it. She grunted from the pain and the effort. She was still wearing the panties, which needed to be removed. I lifted one thigh and butt cheek, then another, inching the panties off until they were far enough away for her to do her business. She did, wiped with her good hand, and then held her arm out for me to put her back on the bed. This was easier—not because I was any better at it, but because the bed was higher and bigger and softer if I set her down too hard. We inched those panties back up; I lifted her legs onto the bed, covered her with her sheet, and put the potty back at the foot of the bed. I don't remember if I cleaned it first or not. I don't remember where the toilet paper went or if there was a box of baby wipes at the bedside. What I remember is that we sat together, holding hands.

Jay came home with groceries. When I told him

about our adventure, he showed me how to position my legs and feet to get a good lift—if it ever happened again. It didn't. Three days later I flew back home, and a week after that, she was gone.

Gone. A word so seemingly final and yet so wispy on the inside, so inconclusive at its end. Even after her spirit had fled her traitorous earthly shell, I held onto pieces of her—brushed her hair down my daughter's back, put rings on my fingers that were just like her own, noticed stacks of books on the table beside my bed, standing in a precarious, but loved, pile, as hers always had.

And I found her in that laugh. Even as I write this, I can hear it. Mom hadn't laughed much in the last years of her life—almost not at all in those last times. And yet there it was for me—that little gift as we wobbled next to a plastic adult toilet, pushing away all that was cruel and unfair about her illness, letting it know it couldn't have us, not all the way. Laughing for just a moment in the face of impending death; and hugging.

About the Author

Jean Knight Pace is the author of the YA fantasy novels, *Grey Stone* and *Grey Lore*. She has also had essays and short stories published in *Puerto del Sol, The Lakeview Review, Crucible,* and other literary magazines. She lives in Indiana with her husband, four children, six ducks, and a cat. You can find more about her at jeanknightpace.com.

www.ingramcontent.com/pod-product-compliance
Lightning Source LLC
Chambersburg PA
CBHW030459010526
44118CB00011B/1015